16167

E
666
MIT

Mitgutsch, Ali

From sand to glass

$6.95

DATE			

From Sand to Glass

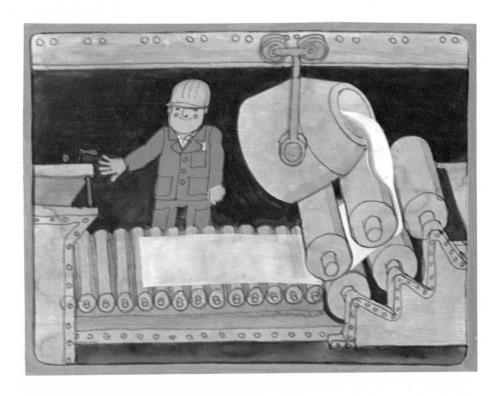

From Sand
to Glass

Ali Mitgutsch

 Carolrhoda Books, Inc., Minneapolis

First published in the United States of America 1981 by
Carolrhoda Books, Inc. All English language rights reserved.

Original edition © 1972 by Sellier Verlag GmbH, Eching bei München,
West Germany, under the title VOM SAND ZUM GLAS.
Revised English text © 1981 by Carolrhoda Books, Inc.
Illustrations © 1972 by Sellier Verlag GmbH.

Manufactured in the United States of America

LIBRARY OF CONGRESS CATALOGING IN PUBLICATION DATA

Mitgutsch, Ali.
  From sand to glass.

    (A Carolrhoda start to finish book)
    First published under title: Vom Sand zum Glas.
    SUMMARY: Describes the process of glassmaking
from the melting of sand in a furnace with soda, lime,
and recycled glass to the molten glass that is blown
into bottles and jars and rolled into window panes.

    1. Glass manufacture—Juvenile literature. [1. Glass
manufacture] I. Title.

TP857.3.M5513   1981   666'.1   80-29572
ISBN 0-87614-162-9

        2 3 4 5 6 7 8 9 10 86 85 84 83 82

From Sand to Glass

Glass is made from sand.

First the sand is scooped out of the ground and loaded into trucks.

The trucks take the sand to a glass factory.
Or they may take the sand to a train
and the train will take it to the factory.
A glass factory is called a **glassworks**.

At the glassworks
the sand is poured into huge furnaces
with soda, lime, and **cullet**.
Cullet is recycled glass
that has been broken into tiny pieces.
Then the furnace is turned on.

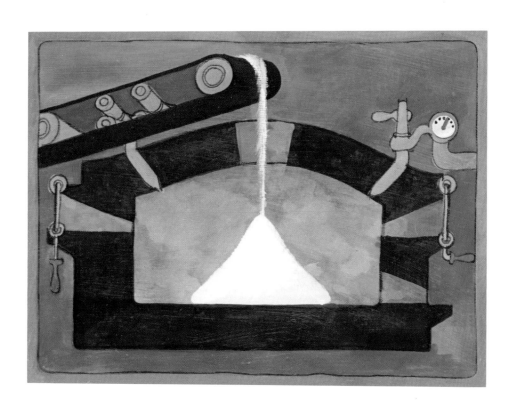

Inside the furnace the temperature gets very hot.

The sand mixture melts together.

It becomes soft and gooey like honey.

This mixture is called **molten glass**.

The molten glass will harden into glass as it cools off.

Before it has hardened, the molten glass must be shaped.

One end of a long iron pipe is dipped into the molten glass.

A small glob will stick to the pipe.

A **glassblower** then blows gently through the pipe,

and the molten glass blows up like a balloon.

The glassblower turns the pipe around as he blows.

This is how he shapes the object he is making.

When the object is the right size,

the glassblower breaks it off the end of the pipe

and sets it aside to cool.

Windows are also made from molten glass,
but they are not made by a glassblower.
The soft glass is poured into a machine with huge rollers.
After the molten glass has been flattened by the rollers,
it is cooled and cut into window-size pieces.

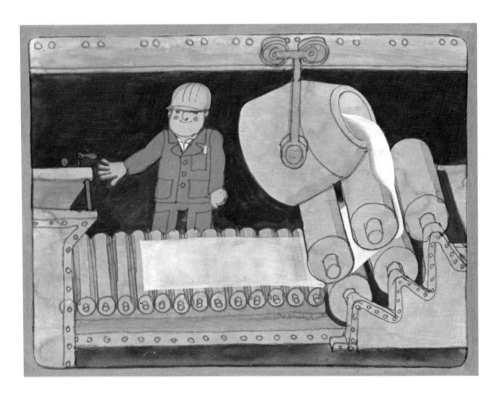

Now the glass is ready to be shipped.
It must be packed very carefully so it won't break.
It might be shipped to a construction company
or a bottling company or a chemical company
or an automobile manufacturer.
These are just a few of the businesses
that depend on glass.

Think of all the glass in your life.
Glass bottles, glass dishes,
glass windows, glass bowls.
Isn't it amazing
that all of it started out as sand!

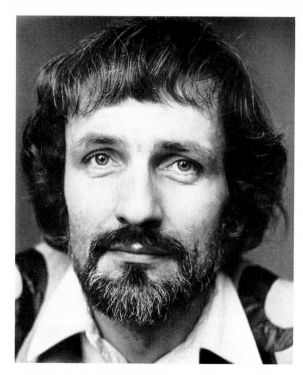

Ali
Mitgutsch

ALI MITGUTSCH is one of Germany's best-known children's book illustrators. He is a devoted world traveler, and many of his book ideas have taken shape during his travels. Perhaps this is why they have such international appeal. Mr. Mitgutsch's books have been published in 22 countries and are enjoyed by thousands of readers around the world.

Ali Mitgutsch lives with his wife and three children in Schwabing, the artists' quarter in Munich. The Mitgutsch family also enjoys spending time on their farm in the Bavarian countryside.

THE CAROLRHODA

>>> START

TO FINISH >>>

BOOKS